*M*Y, OH MY, so you are afraid to start? Do you know everyone is, even we professionals are from time to time, but we have a job that must be out, say next Wednesday and we get at it because we may have a family that has gotten into the habit of eating three times a day or the payment on the house or car may be coming up. So it is a must for the professional but you may be painting for fun so this fear of making a mistake has a greater influence over you and you may say to yourself "I'm not inspired today" or "I don't think I have a talent for painting", or four dozen other excuses one can make to get out of starting.

Another great mistake is choosing a subject that is far too advanced for your ability at this moment and another that you are expected to originate your first painting. A good copy of a painting you like is much better than anything you can think up on your own.

If you must work from life pick just a single flower, vegetable, fruit or vase, draw carefully and paint. This will be your start and you will not say "I can't" on your first or five hundredth try. Jump in the pool, get your feet wet and keep them damp. Thousands have thanked my books for showing them the way to something they have wanted to do for years and at last here you are trying and may you never put your materials away because if you do you are slamming the door on a very wonderful therapy that will blot out all troubles and worries and give you a satisfaction and appreciation that nothing else in the world will do — and for so little. Read Bill Mooney's letter in the 4th vol. of "How and What to Paint" magazine, page 18. He lives in Australia and after an accident left him paralyzed from a broken neck he now paints by holding the brush in his mouth. If we have our health can anyone's problems be as great as his? We all have so much to be thankful for. I know I do. Shall we start, say on this flower? Fine, and may you never stop—only, of course, to eat, sleep and have a good time.

Sincerely yours,

Walter Foster

THE YELLOW Roses give you a subject colorful but not too hard. It will take thought and a good drawing. If using watercolor use waterproof India ink for background, then you can use color over it without it running. Leave white paper if you can, if not use white opaque for highlights. These Roses were painted in watercolors on illustration board. You can do them in oils on canvas board or try plastic colors on canvas or illustration board. Do not be afraid to try since that is the real way to learn.

⒐NE GREAT advantage in working from photos is that they do not move, fade or die. Most artists work from photos. I know I have for years. A well-rounded artist is one that can and does work from life, photos and can draw from any subject that he or she may need in the picture. It is too bad that so many start by taking on all the phony beliefs that people pass on to them, such as "never copy a picture, you will take on that artist's style and you are ruined", or the one that stops so many promising beginners "never copy—always originate". The next time this is said to you ask what they have originated.

CADMIUM RED LIGHT & WHITE plus PERMANENT GREEN LIGHT

CADMIUM YELLOW MEDIUM & WHITE plus WINSOR VIOLET

ULTRAMARINE BLUE & WHITE plus CADMIUM ORANGE

PERMANENT GREEN LIGHT & WHITE plus CADMIUM RED LIGHT

Walter Foster

AS YOU can see in step one you have placement of the two main flowers. This is the same whether they are flowers, apples, vase or figurines and if you will think this out on all painting or drawing you do it will become a habit that will be of the greatest help to you. Be definite, do not make scratchy lines. Think, then draw. As you work on your painting you may want to outline the flowers as I have done instead of painting them in detail. The hardest part is knowing how to start and that is why this and others pictured are not completed. Now it is up to you to try. This was 18" x 24" and painted with the new Acrylic paints.

The step drawings leading up to the finished drawing must be followed closely to receive the most good out of this and other studies, if you revert back to your hit-and-miss way, or as my little girl once said when I was showing her how to use arm movement "Do they pay you for showing them this?" I said "yes." She pinches up her little fingers and said "I believe I like my system the best." Well, she has made a good housewife and mother and a grand pal so what's the difference.

It is well to have a thick blotter and cloth to take up the excess color.

No. 3—After adding leaves and completing drawing of flowers add background and complete yellow wash.

No. 4—After yellow wash dries add orange and then red orange.

No. 5—Add red-violet and violet. If you have put on too much color add extra clear water, squeeze out your large brush and it will soak up extra color, or use a blotter. To darken the red add violet over the red.

No. 2—After you have a good drawing of the flowers as shown, you may start with first wash of yellow orange.

No. 1—First you decide the size you want the picture, divide the sides, top and bottom into thirds. This will give you four crosses to place the main object of interest on any one of these crosses so you will not center it and have a poor composition.

W. T. F.

Procrastination is one of our greatest faults along with expecting too much of ourselves at the start of a new venture such as art of any kind. We buy a book, materials, etc. and make a few swipes at the paper, see that it does not look like the original and quit, and it never occurs to you that the artist has been at it for years so should be able to do quite a bit better than you just starting. Just remember this on all of your trying and do not be discouraged if your efforts do not look as good at the start. That is why I have made all of these step drawings so you can sneak up on it gradually and have much better results, even if you think your system *is* better than mine.

A single flower with a bud or so and a few leaves is a big enough problem for anyone. It isn't necessary to hold to either coloring or form. I show, in the left hand corner at the bottom, the flower has been turned around so it will go into a vertical panel. The fun of all painting is to think for yourself. Do as you please and if you think wrong you learn more. This sounds off base but it surely makes sense. Try it and see.

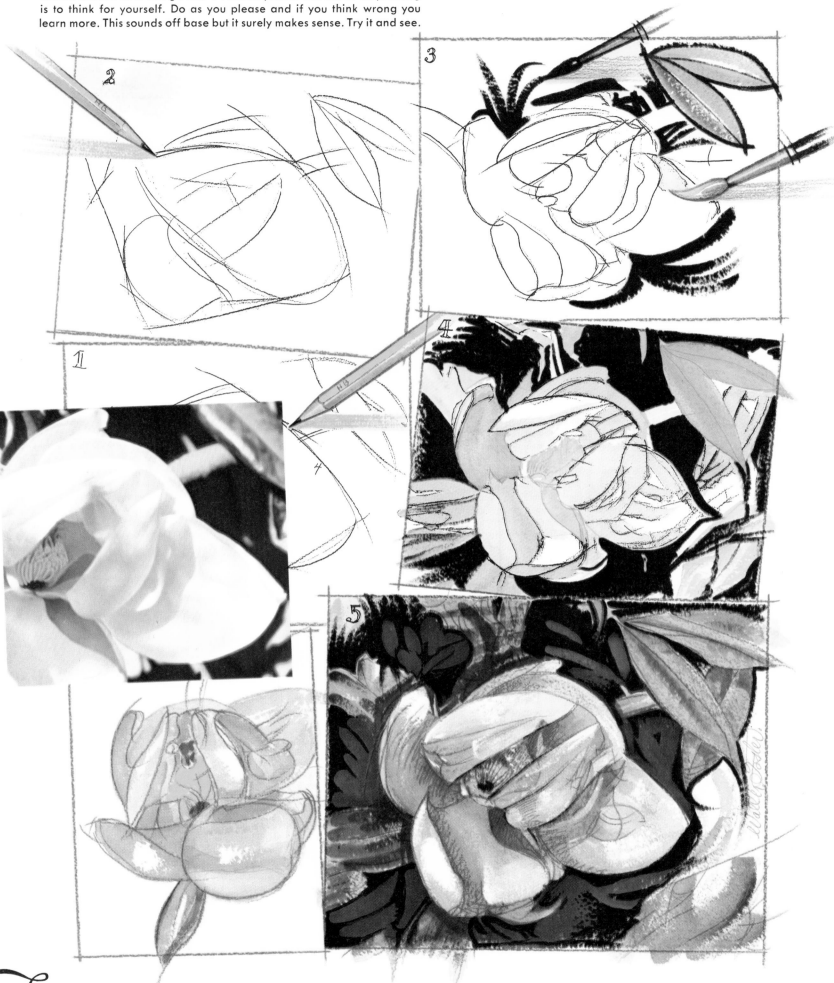

THERE ARE so many things you can do with different flowers as objects if you can draw well which comes only with lots of practice—having a rich uncle or aunt has nothing to do with it. The reason they have you do abstract or so called modern paintings is the lack of knowing how to draw. The real abstract or moderns are made by artists who can draw as well as paint. There are no shortcuts to good painting and the best of artists paint many passable, poor and good paintings so do not be peeved at yourself if a few of your efforts do not turn out as well as you had expected.

𝒫AINTING FROM a beautiful photo like this is such a help. I have held close to the picture in my step drawings and final painting but if doing this for sale I would shift the flowers around so they would not be recognized as being taken from this photo or better still I would draw and paint from the real flowers. If you learn to draw well you will find it just as easy to draw from the still life of the real flower as a photo or you can combine both. Try it. O.K.?

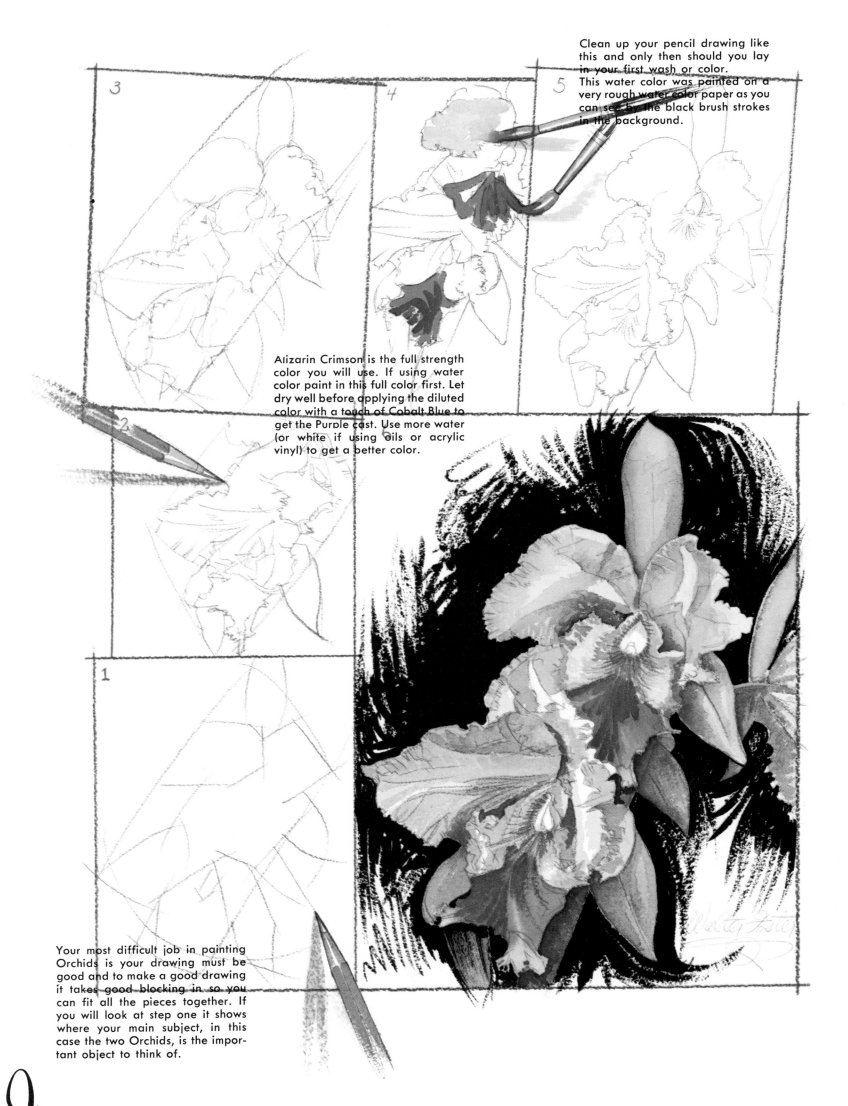

Clean up your pencil drawing like this and only then should you lay in your first wash or color.
This water color was painted on a very rough water color paper as you can see by the black brush strokes in the background.

Alizarin Crimson is the full strength color you will use. If using water color paint in this full color first. Let dry well before applying the diluted color with a touch of Cobalt Blue to get the Purple cast. Use more water (or white if using oils or acrylic vinyl) to get a better color.

Your most difficult job in painting Orchids is your drawing must be good and to make a good drawing it takes good blocking in so you can fit all the pieces together. If you will look at step one it shows where your main subject, in this case the two Orchids, is the important object to think of.

I LIKE to have my paper or board so I can turn it around. It is much easier to work on and your brush strokes will be freer. Remember you can always put another darker wash over your drawing. Try dragging your brush over a lighter color so it can show through and if you want your painting to LOOK like a painting—SIMPLIFY! Yes, leave out whatever you feel does not help or is not necessary. Keep building on your drawing. Work all over it. Do not finish one spot at a time. For contrast darken parts of your picture that will make the edges stand out. Brighten any colors that you feel will bring out the flower. No, you should not stick to the exact color of the picture. Liven it up, if not, why not just take the colored photo?

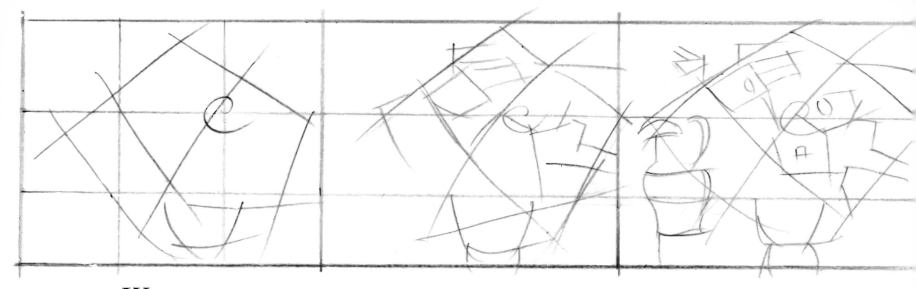

*W*HEN painting flowers and until you have had quite a bit of experience it is best to carry your step-drawings in pencil or charcoal, much farther than the first step here. I show different stages—so choose the one that suits you the best. You will find this out by trying. Just looking won't help you a bit. Shall we start?

The effect you obtain with pastels depends largely upon the surface of the papers you choose. in the color reproductions below, you will find different papers, with effects you will get using colored pencils, hard pastels and soft pastels.

This row is on cold pressed (C.P.) illustration board. ←

This row is on hot pressed (H.P.) illustration board. ←

This row is on hot pressed (H.P.) Bristol board. ←

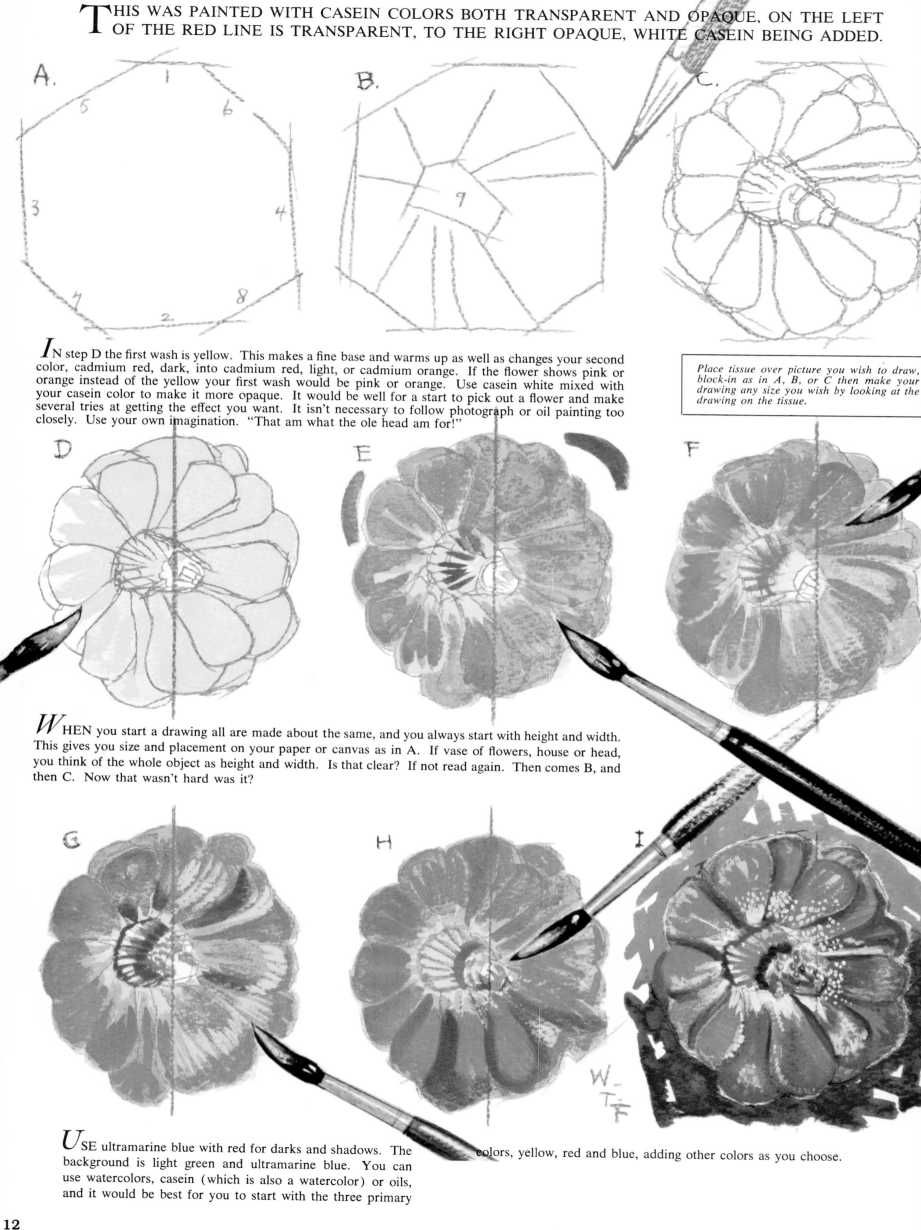

THIS WAS PAINTED WITH CASEIN COLORS BOTH TRANSPARENT AND OPAQUE, ON THE LEFT OF THE RED LINE IS TRANSPARENT, TO THE RIGHT OPAQUE, WHITE CASEIN BEING ADDED.

A.

B.

C.

IN step D the first wash is yellow. This makes a fine base and warms up as well as changes your second color, cadmium red, dark, into cadmium red, light, or cadmium orange. If the flower shows pink or orange instead of the yellow your first wash would be pink or orange. Use casein white mixed with your casein color to make it more opaque. It would be well for a start to pick out a flower and make several tries at getting the effect you want. It isn't necessary to follow photograph or oil painting too closely. Use your own imagination. "That am what the ole head am for!"

Place tissue over picture you wish to draw, block-in as in A, B, or C then make your drawing any size you wish by looking at the drawing on the tissue.

D

E

F

WHEN you start a drawing all are made about the same, and you always start with height and width. This gives you size and placement on your paper or canvas as in A. If vase of flowers, house or head, you think of the whole object as height and width. Is that clear? If not read again. Then comes B, and then C. Now that wasn't hard was it?

G

H

I

W-
T-
F

USE ultramarine blue with red for darks and shadows. The background is light green and ultramarine blue. You can use watercolors, casein (which is also a watercolor) or oils, and it would be best for you to start with the three primary colors, yellow, red and blue, adding other colors as you choose.

Now use your No. 6 Watercolor Brush. Wet flower with clear water, let stand until the water no longer shows.

The poppy is now ready for the coat of yellow—and let dry. Second step, use carmine. Third step, add blue for shadows. Fourth step, intensify your red, yellow and blue for your center, outline and shadows. Try several times until it is clear to you just what has happened.

A good palette. You can add more colors if you wish.

Note: These colors may vary, so go by name rather than by color chart.

1 Lemon or Cadmium Yellow
2 Cadmium Yellow Med.
3 Cadmium Yellow Deep
4 Yellow Ochre
5 Cadmium Orange
6 Vermilion Deep
7 Carmine Red
8 Crimson Lake
9 Light Red
10 Raw Sienna
11 Burnt Umber
12 Van Dyke Brown
13 Permanent Green
14 Emerald Green
15 Sap Green
16 Hooker Green
17 Violet
18 Ultramarine Blue
19 Prussian Blue
20 Ivory Black

Buy at your nearest dealer in Artist Materials.

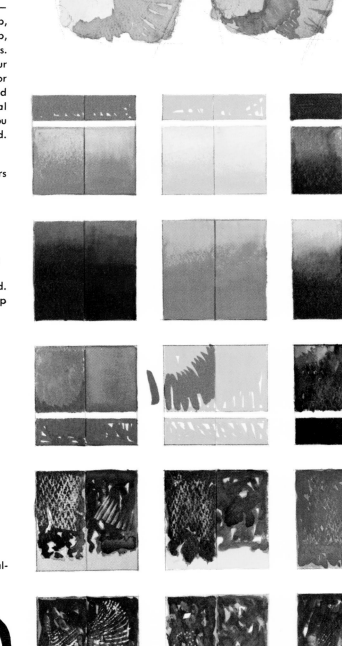

Omitting all other colors from your painting except Red, Yellow and Blue would not create as much of a hardship as you might think.

☆   ☆   ☆

The poppy, leaves, pods, as well as the shadows and squares were painted with these three colors, and I would like to have you think of all other colors as HELPER COLORS, using them only when you cannot obtain the desired colors, tints or grays with your three primary colors. As long as you hold to your Red, Yellow and Blue, your watercolor will be clean, free from muddiness and using the same care with your drawing, you will obtain a crisp, clear-cut painting of any subject you wish to do. Try it and good going.

So AS not to take up four pages with materials you will use, I have placed all on one page, so take your choice—to the right if you wish to work in Oils—then right and at the bottom for Water Colors, and underneath this you have Pastels, colored pencils and general material you will use.

Try one at a time. I show flowers in all mediums and you can paint any and all in your chosen medium, although it may be shown in another medium. And, a word about Casein or Gouache or Tempera, which are applied about the same. You thin with water and apply a great deal like Oil Paint, using watercolor brushes and some artists use oil brushes, too. It may be of interest to you, that on the covers of several of my books I have used the combination of Casein and Pastels. Sure, they work fine together. Apply Casein first then the Pastels over. Use cold-pressed illustration board.

If IN DOUBT AS TO WHETHER YOUR MEDIUM IS WATER COLOR, OILS OR PASTELS, TRY THEM ALL. I FIND THAT IF YOU KNOW SOMETHING ABOUT EACH, THE SUBJECT YOU CHOOSE WILL SUGGEST WHICH MEDIUM IS BEST. BY THE WAY, CAN YOU DRAW WELL? DO NOT NEGLECT THIS PART OF YOUR TRAINING.

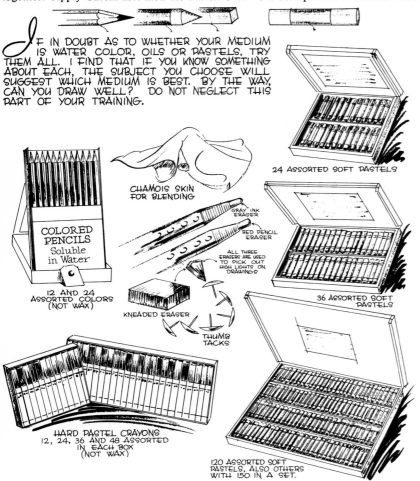

CHAMOIS SKIN FOR BLENDING

GRAY INK ERASER

RED PENCIL ERASER

ALL THREE ERASERS ARE USED TO PICK OUT HIGH LIGHTS ON DRAWINGS.

KNEADED ERASER

THUMB TACKS

COLORED PENCILS Soluble in Water

12 AND 24 ASSORTED COLORS (NOT WAX)

24 ASSORTED SOFT PASTELS

36 ASSORTED SOFT PASTELS

HARD PASTEL CRAYONS 12, 24, 36 AND 48 ASSORTED IN EACH BOX (NOT WAX)

120 ASSORTED SOFT PASTELS, ALSO OTHERS WITH 150 IN A SET.

PALETTE KNIVES

PAINTING KNIVES

ARM PALETTS (IF LEFT HANDED TELL THE ART DEALER)

CUPS FOR OIL AND TURPENTINE

STUDIO EASEL

ARTISTS' OIL COLOR OUTFIT

SKETCHING EASEL

Buy ONLY THE BEST MATERIALS AND TAKE GOOD CARE OF THEM. CHEAP TOOLS ARE OF LITTLE VALUE TO A BEGINNER OR PROFESSIONAL ~~~ PERSONALLY I LIKE A GOOD RED SABLE WATERCOLOR BRUSH FOR BLOCKING-IN IN OILS.

SABLE BRUSHES

LARGE FLAT BRISTLE BRUSH FOR PAINTING FLAT COAT ON MASONITE OR CANVAS

LONG FLAT BRISTLE BRUSHES

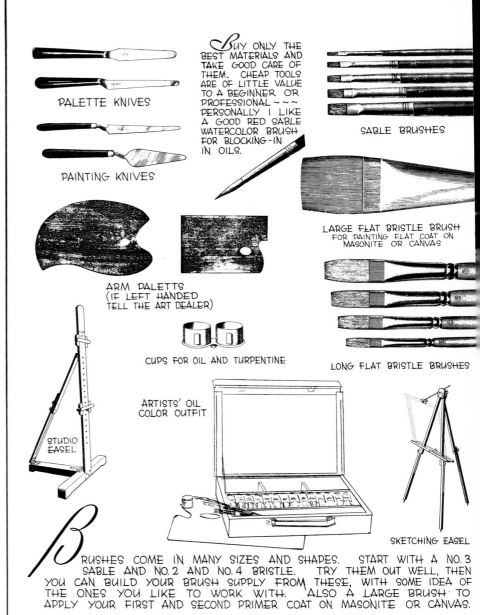

Brushes COME IN MANY SIZES AND SHAPES. START WITH A NO. 3 SABLE AND NO. 2 AND NO. 4 BRISTLE. TRY THEM OUT WELL, THEN YOU CAN BUILD YOUR BRUSH SUPPLY FROM THESE, WITH SOME IDEA OF THE ONES YOU LIKE TO WORK WITH. ALSO A LARGE BRUSH TO APPLY YOUR FIRST AND SECOND PRIMER COAT ON MASONITE OR CANVAS.

FELT STUMP

FELT, PAPER OR LEATHER STUMP FOR BLENDING

SAND PAPER BLOCK FOR POINTING CHARCOAL AND PENCILS

FIXATIF AND ATOMIZERS

DUSTING BRUSH

CRAYON HOLDER

WILLOW CHARCOAL STICK

COMPRESSED CHARCOAL

CHARCOAL PENCIL

STUDIO EASEL WITH DRAWING BOARD

T-SQUARE IS NEEDED TO SQUARE YOU DRAWING

SKETCHING EASEL AND LIGHT PLYWOOD DRAWING BOARD

A SMOOTH DRAWING BOARD IS A MUST

WHEN APPLYING FIXATIF, STAND AWAY FROM YOUR PICTURE 20 TO 24 INCHES. DO NOT FLOOD IT ON AND LET DRY WELL BEFORE ADDING MORE. IN COLOR WORK IT IS ADVISABLE TO SET YOUR COLORS SEVERAL TIMES DURING THE MAKING OF A PICTURE. WHEN COMPLETING, APPLY LITTLE OR NO FIXATIF. THIS WILL GIVE IT A FRESH LOOK BECAUSE FIXATIF, AT ITS BEST, DULLS YOUR COLORS. I PREFER USING GLASS TO FIXATIF AND IT SHOULD BE FRAMED SO THERE WILL BE 1/4 OF AN INCH BETWEEN PICTURE AND GLASS.

A CHAIR, TURNED UPSIDE DOWN, MAKES A GOOD EASEL. PUT IT ON A LOW TABLE IF YOU WISH TO STAND UP, OF COURSE, AN ADJUSTABLE EASEL IS BEST.

This IS A MORE COMPLETE LIST IF YOU WISH TO START IN WELL EQUIPPED FOR SKETCHING TRIPS, AS WELL AS STUDIO USE ~~~~~~

20 ASSORTED PASTELS, SOFT.
24 ASSORTED PASTELS, HARD.
12 ASSORTED PENCILS.
DRAWING BOARDS.
STUDIO AND SKETCHING EASEL.
T-SQUARE.
FIXATIF AND ATOMIZER.
6 SHEETS OF ASSORTED PASTEL AND CHARCOAL PAPER.

DRAFTSMAN'S DUSTING BRUSH.
6 THUMB TACKS.
1 ROLL OF SCOTCH TAPE.
2 PENCIL SHAPED ERASERS, HARD AND SOFT.
1 KNEADED RUBBER ERASER.
1 CHAMOIS SKIN.
6 ASSORTED STUMPS, LARGE AND SMALL.

Materials YOU WILL NEED

YOUR LOCAL ART STORE CAN SUPPLY YOU.

DO NOT BUY POOR OR CHEAP BRUSHES

FOR YOUR PRACTICE WORK, USE A WATER COLOR PAD OR BLOCK AND STUDENTS WATER COLOR PAPER, BUT IF YOU CAN BUY ILLUSTRATION BOARD, IT IS BEST, BECAUSE THERE IS NO WARPING. IT COMES IN HOT PRESSED (HP) SMOOTH AND COLD PRESSED (C.P.) ROUGH.

SMOOTH 22" X 30"
ROUGH 22" X 30"
EXTRA ROUGH 22" X 30"
ILLUSTRATION BOARD 20" X 30" 30" X 40"

START WITH A NO. 3 AND A NO. 6 RED SABLE BRUSHES. THE NO. 12 BRUSH IS QUITE EXPENSIVE. DO NOT BUY UNTIL YOU ARE QUITE SURE YOU INTEND KEEPING UP YOUR PAINTING.

RED SABLES

NO. 12 RED SABLE

FLAT WASH BRUSH FINE QUALITY

GOOD FOR LARGE WASHES BUT I PREFER A NO. 12 BRUSH

A BOX OF COLORED PENCILS OR CRAYONS TO OUTLINE AND ACCENTUATE YOUR DRAWING.

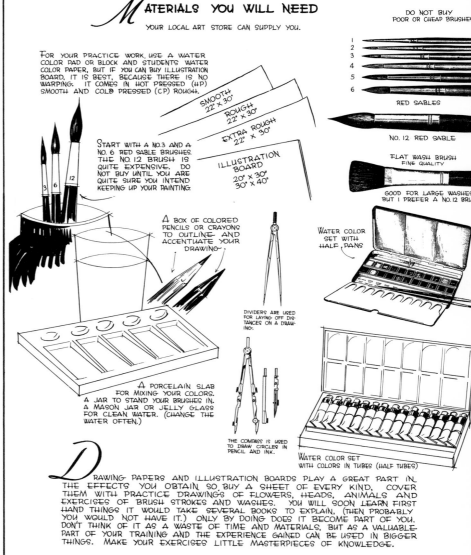

WATER COLOR SET WITH HALF PANS

DIVIDERS ARE USED FOR LAYING OFF DISTANCES ON A DRAWING.

A PORCELAIN SLAB FOR MIXING YOUR COLORS. A JAR TO STAND YOUR BRUSHES IN. A MASON JAR OR JELLY GLASS FOR CLEAN WATER. (CHANGE THE WATER OFTEN.)

THE COMPASS IS USED TO DRAW CIRCLES IN PENCIL AND INK.

WATER COLOR SET WITH COLORS IN TUBES (HALF TUBES)

Drawing PAPERS AND ILLUSTRATION BOARDS PLAY A GREAT PART IN THE EFFECTS YOU OBTAIN SO, BUY A SHEET OF EVERY KIND, COVER THEM WITH PRACTICE DRAWINGS OF FLOWERS, HEADS, ANIMALS AND EXERCISES OF BRUSH STROKES AND WASHES. YOU WILL SOON LEARN FIRST HAND THINGS IT WOULD TAKE SEVERAL BOOKS TO EXPLAIN. (THEN PROBABLY YOU WOULD NOT HAVE IT.) ONLY BY DOING IT DOES IT BECOME PART OF YOU. DON'T THINK OF IT AS A WASTE OF TIME AND MATERIALS, BUT AS A VALUABLE PART OF YOUR TRAINING AND THE EXPERIENCE GAINED CAN BE USED IN BIGGER THINGS. MAKE YOUR EXERCISES LITTLE MASTERPIECES OF KNOWLEDGE.

SEE COLOR WHEEL
CLOCKWISE OUTER CIRCLE

YELLOW
*Cadmium Yellow

YELLOW GREEN
or
PERMANENT GREEN
Two parts Cadmium
Yellow
One Part Ultramarine
Blue

GREEN
Half Yellow
Half Blue

BLUE GREEN
VIRIDIAN
One part Yellow
Two parts Blue

BLUE
*ULTRAMARINE BLUE
Ultramarine Blue

BLUE VIOLET
Two parts Blue
One part Red

VIOLET
One half Blue
One half Red

RED VIOLET
Two parts Red
One part Blue

RED
*Cadmium Red
(medium)

RED ORANGE
Two parts Red
One part Yellow

ORANGE
One half Red
One half Yellow

YELLOW ORANGE
Two parts Yellow
One part Red

**INNER COLOR WHEEL
CLOCKWISE**

CITRON
One half Orange
One half Green

YELLOW and BLUE
As you can see by
arrows is a mixture of
half yellow and half
blue

OLIVE
Green and Violet mixed

RED and BLUE
Half Blue
Half Red

RUSSET
Half Orange
Half Violet

YELLOW and RED
Half Cadmium Yellow
Half Cadmium Red

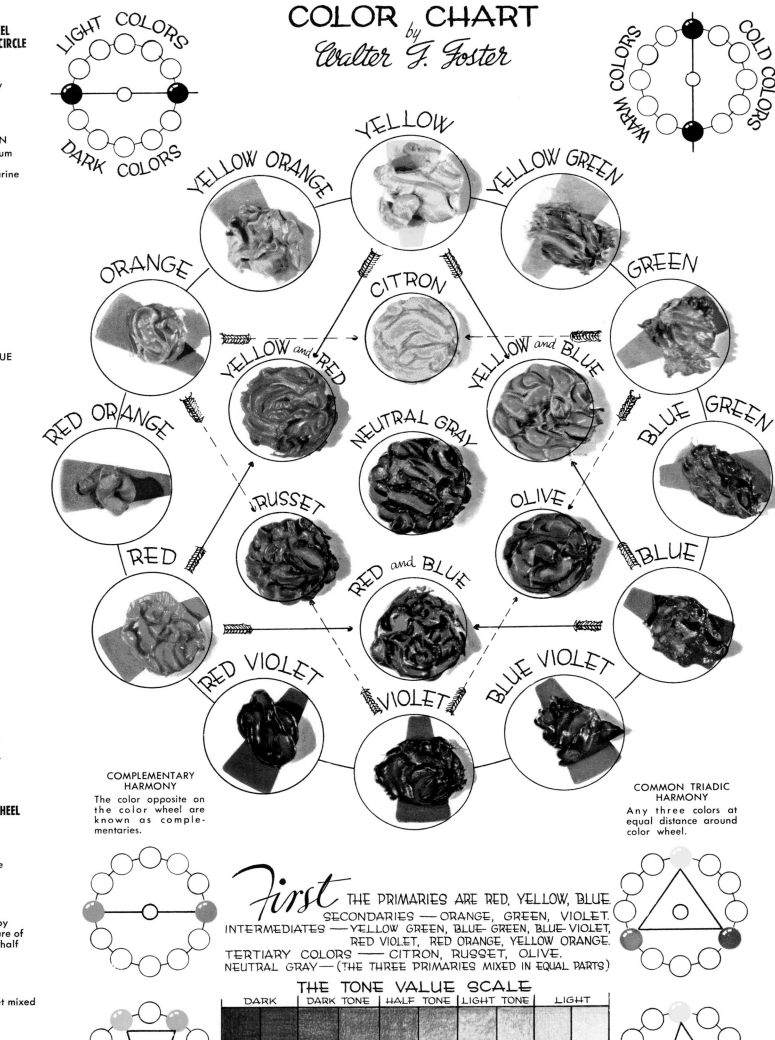

LIGHT COLORS
DARK COLORS

WARM COLORS
COLD COLORS

YELLOW ORANGE — YELLOW — YELLOW GREEN
CITRON
ORANGE — YELLOW and RED — YELLOW and BLUE — GREEN
RED ORANGE — NEUTRAL GRAY — BLUE GREEN
RUSSET — OLIVE
RED — RED and BLUE — BLUE
RED VIOLET — VIOLET — BLUE VIOLET

COMPLEMENTARY HARMONY
The color opposite on
the color wheel are
known as comple-
mentaries.

**COMMON TRIADIC
HARMONY**
Any three colors at
equal distance around
color wheel.

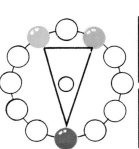

First THE PRIMARIES ARE RED, YELLOW, BLUE.
SECONDARIES — ORANGE, GREEN, VIOLET.
INTERMEDIATES — YELLOW GREEN, BLUE-GREEN, BLUE-VIOLET,
RED VIOLET, RED ORANGE, YELLOW ORANGE.
TERTIARY COLORS — CITRON, RUSSET, OLIVE.
NEUTRAL GRAY — (THE THREE PRIMARIES MIXED IN EQUAL PARTS)

THE TONE VALUE SCALE

DARK	DARK TONE	HALF TONE	LIGHT TONE	LIGHT

SPLIT COMPLEMENTARY
HARMONY

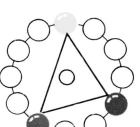

HARMONIOUS
COLOR BALANCE

MANY COLOR CHARTS OR COLOR WHEELS HAVE CARDBOARD
OR PLASTIC DIALS, YOU CAN MAKE YOUR OWN AND USE
ON THIS CHART. THE THREE SHAPES (ONE TO LEFT AND
TWO TO RIGHT) CAN BE USED, JUST MAKE THEM LARGER.
STICK PIN IN CENTER AND YOU HAVE SAVED $1.00 ~ ~ ~ ~
ISN'T THAT NICE.

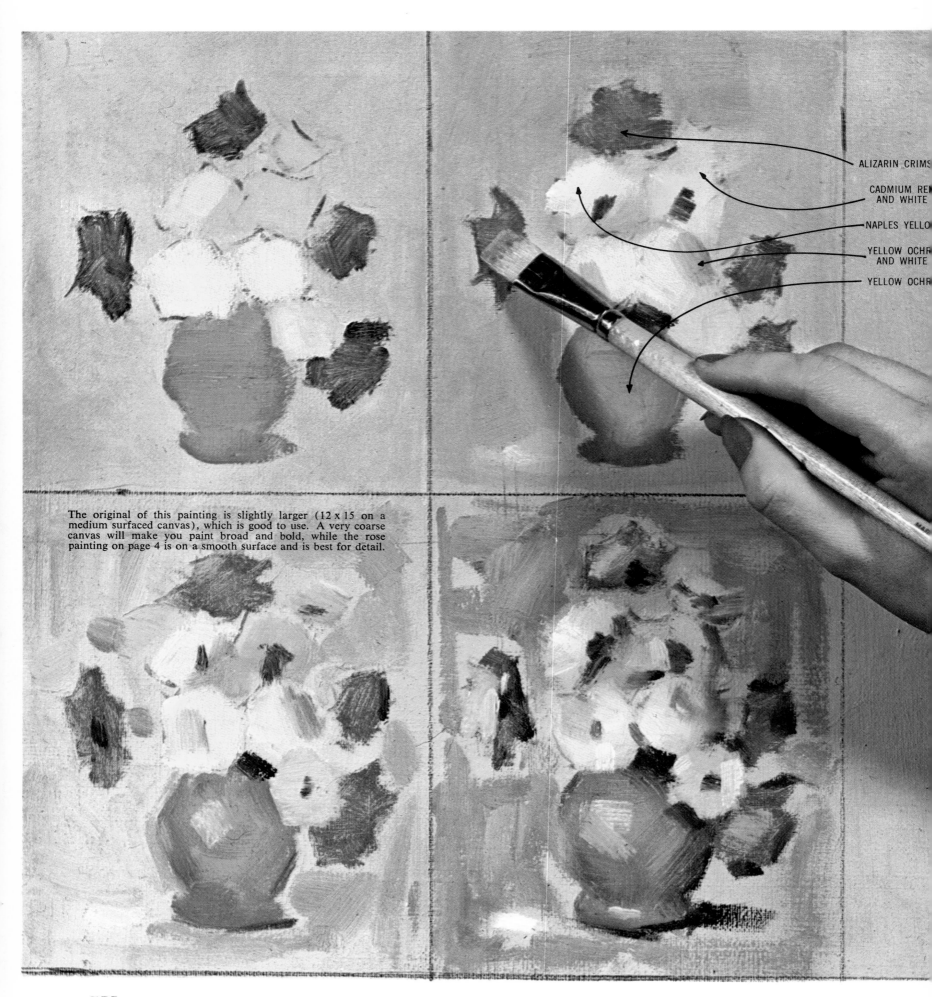

ALIZARIN CRIMS

CADMIUM REI
AND WHITE

NAPLES YELLO

YELLOW OCHR
AND WHITE

YELLOW OCHR

The original of this painting is slightly larger (12 x 15 on a medium surfaced canvas), which is good to use. A very coarse canvas will make you paint broad and bold, while the rose painting on page 4 is on a smooth surface and is best for detail.

*W*HEN you try painting any of these paintings do not be disturbed if yours is not like the one you work from. This is a good sign, a sign that you can develop an individuality of your own. Just keep painting. One must do enough painting to awaken the little inner voice in each one of us that says yes or no, same as putting your foot on the brake or the gas. We act through experiences we have had, learned through practice, such as making flowers your way, using your favorite color, etc. This all goes to make your work individual, and if you follow this little voice and develop it, it will take you on a wonderful journey through this life.

*I*f just starting, start in one single petal flowers like Hollyhocks, single roses, etc. and on flower or leaf at a time. The more difficult the subject the quicker one becomes discouraged never blaming it on the choice of subject but feeling that you are not capable of doing the subject. Do *not* blame yourself, just pick out something that you can do. Patience and understanding of one's self is quite an accomplishment and if practiced reflects our good qualities to others.

*A*s you can see in step 1 the branch and picture is built on this same reverse curve turned sidewise that I made for the artists in Hong Kong and the whole picture is confined inside of the three lines built around this line of *rhythm*. The bird is placed on the one line while the flowers are on the lower for good composition. This gives a beautifully balanced picture with interest in all parts with the branch leading up to the bird, and as you will note the writing and signature also plays an important part in the composition of their pictures. The stamen and pollen buds were put in last with opaque water colors. See print on next page. The original is 16 x 20. Try making this for a change.

The Orientals as well as many others have gone into the so-called modern trend which is too bad and instead of an individual beauty it all looks alike, clear around this old globe of ours. In Japan one of the best oriental painters is an American woman, the daughter-in-law of my good friend Lynn Bogue Hunt. (see his Bird book). My visit and dinner with the Hunts in Japan was one of the highlights of my last trip there. The above is an original I bought in Hong Kong six years ago and I love its freedom, simplicity and interesting composition.

CHINESE PAINTINGS such as these are made only after practicing and memorizing the many different forms and brush strokes. If you are interested ask to see the Chows' book on "AN EASY WAY TO DO CHINESE PAINTING" #69. It will show you the way but the "easy" should have been left out. It is easy to the Chows but remember they've been at it for many years. It is a most interesting book. Also we have a movie showing the Chows at work with their students.

IF YOU wish to try painting these two, or the one on page 19, I suggest you follow my step drawing on page 18 which is the way I would paint pictures like these—make your pencil drawing first, then fill in the penciled lines or perhaps you want to try your own way which is fine too. But at least try.
These originals are 19" x 24" watercolors and beautiful to frame.

THIS STILL LIFE is one of Leon Franks' more finished paintings. Yes, more in the traditional style, one you can live with for years and enjoy seeing from day to day. It gives me a sense of pleasure. No guessing as to what it is or what it has to say. It leaves no doubt in one's mind but what Leon knew what he was doing. If you can paint this kind of painting it is always saleable. The size of the original is 20" x 24"—always a good size to paint.

ANOTHER of Leon Franks' still life. It is very busy with many things to look at and would be a picture people would notice more and talk about but not so easy to live with as the one above. It takes all kinds to please all kinds of people so in your paintings try for something new as Leon always does. This will only come to you through many, many paintings. As long as Mr. Franks has been painting they still do not always come easy. I stopped by his studio one evening recently, and he was struggling with one that almost had him down. Ask to see his three books, STILL LIFE #52, "TECHNIQUES IN OILS" #79 and "CLOWNS AND CHARAC-TERS" #62. If you like his work—and who doesn't, you will find step paintings showing how it is done.

THIS IS a lovely still life I bought in Italy. It is the same size as the original. It was done with brush, painting knife and great understanding so you see a painting does not have to be big to have quality. If you wish to try this, pick one or several paintings that show the step painting and do the same step painting for yourself.

THIS STILL LIFE painting is by Maurice Decamps of France and is a very lovely painting. Having painted it broad it is quite easy to live with.

Maurice Décamps

W HEN you get as good at it as Nell you have reached the top. By the way I just received a card from Nell and "Shoshie." She says: "Hi! Aboard the finest of S. S. 'Kungsholm' smooth sailing on the way to Sweden." I did not know when I saw them last that Mary and Igor Gorin and yours truly would be on this same ship in 10 days. Will try and have lots of interesting things to tell you on a new book I have in the making. 'Bye. W.T.F.

THIS is a section, same size, of Nell Walker Warner's beautiful painting shown above, which will give you a good idea of how she has worked out a simple way of painting a difficult subject with brush and painting knife. You can learn much by painting these flowers and studying the real ones. Keep in mind the parts she has left out and how she has suggested details.

THESE step drawings in watercolor will give you an idea of how you build one color over another. Some you let dry and you will have a sharp line, and some where you wish to have your color blend, you work wet. Practice is your best teacher on this. Shall we practice? All roses are much the same as far as painting goes, some you add a little more red than yellow. In watercolor you add water, in oil you add white to make your color lighter, yes for tints.

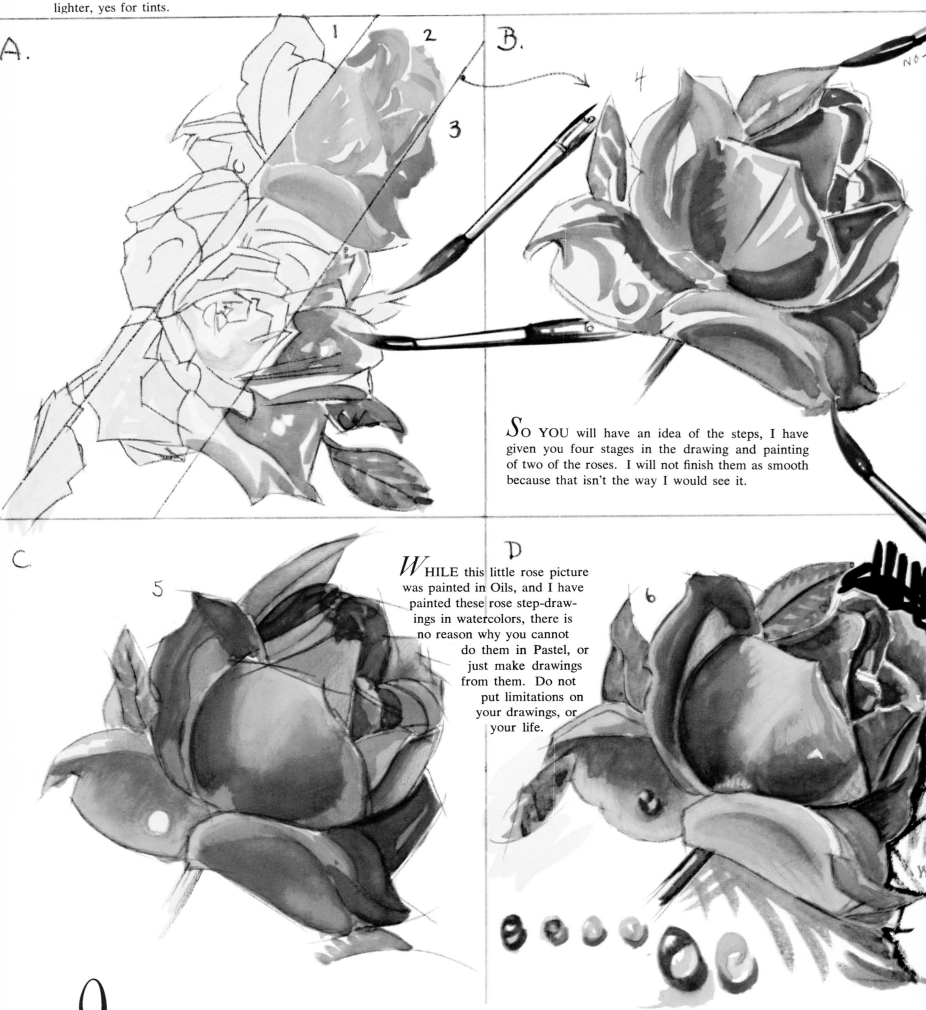

A.

B.

C.

D.

So YOU will have an idea of the steps, I have given you four stages in the drawing and painting of two of the roses. I will not finish them as smooth because that isn't the way I would see it.

WHILE this little rose picture was painted in Oils, and I have painted these rose step-drawings in watercolors, there is no reason why you cannot do them in Pastel, or just make drawings from them. Do not put limitations on your drawings, or your life.

IF YOU are wondering why the dewdrops are oval, it is gravity. Just thought you might like to know. They make a picture of this kind interesting and yet would not fit into a picture painted as broad as the one on page 17 and on pages 23 and 27. I wish to put great stress on the importance of learning how to draw. Drawing from a single flower or a leaf is best at first, then with the right idea of blocking-in you will find both painting and drawing help each. If you have a good seed catalogue or flower arrangement book make many drawings and paintings from them just as studies, because you will want your paintings to be more free and not so set. All this will be a great help with your own painting. Don't be in too much of a hurry to make something original—you did not expect to write a love letter when you were learning your ABC's! Well, same thing. Love? Now that is a nice subject, too.

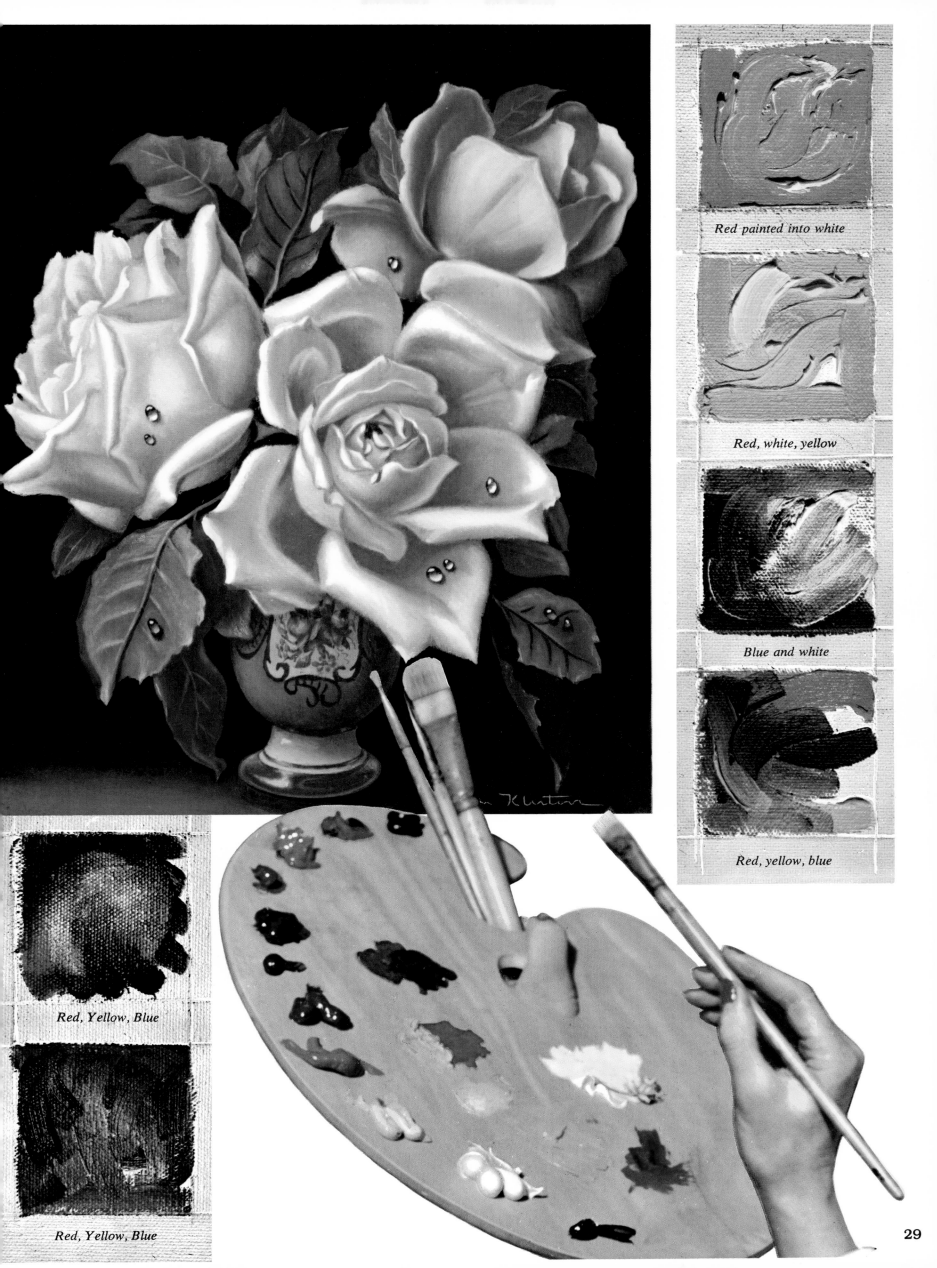

Red painted into white

Red, white, yellow

Blue and white

Red, yellow, blue

Red, Yellow, Blue

Red, Yellow, Blue

𝒯HESE GLADS OF LEON FRANKS are so nice and free I thought you could learn much by trying them.

More Ways To Learn With

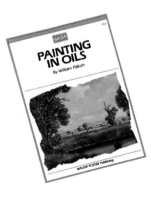

WALTER FOSTER Publishing...
*The most recognized name in art publishing
for more than 74 years!*

Disney Learn To Draw Series

The Walt Disney Company© and Walter Foster Publishing have combined their talents to create this wonderful new series of art books for children.

Each book in the **Disney Learn To Draw Series** features a different set of characters and includes step-by-step instructions and illustrations, fun ways to use action lines, tips on outlining and coloring, and hints on how to create different poses and expressions.

Children will be entertained for hours as they practice drawing their favorite Disney characters—and they'll love showing off their very own "masterpieces"!

Paperback, 32 pages, 10-1/4" x 13-3/4"

How To Series

No matter what the medium or the subject matter, we have a book in our **"How To" Series** to fit every artist's needs.

Filled with step-by-step illustrations of techniques for various media, these books address the full art spectrum—pen and ink, pencil, pastel, charcoal, watercolor, acrylic and oil—and they address all skill levels. Their easy-to-follow instructional style takes the beginning artist through the fundamentals of outlining, shading, form and perspective. And, as each lesson builds on the newly developed skill of the preceding lesson, the books move into the more sophisticated rendering techniques sought by the advanced artist.

Paperback, 32 pages, 10-1/4" x 13-3/4"

Blitz Cartoon Series

This new series is designed for people who just can't stop doodling! Bruce Blitz, creator and host of the Emmy-nominated Public Television series, "*Blitz On Cartooning,*" believes that anyone with desire and a positive attitude can learn to draw—so he has developed these four new books demonstrating fun and easy methods for turning "doodles" into finished drawings, cartoons and comic strips.

The **Blitz Cartoon Series** is perfect for people of all ages who like to draw, but believe they "can't even draw a straight line."

Paperback, 48 pages, 10-1/4" x 13-3/4"

Collector's Series

Each book in the **Collector's Series** contains a selection of some of the most popular books from our "How To" Series—all combined in a high quality, hardcover edition.

Compiled from many of our bestsellers, each of these books begins with the fundamentals of the particular medium—pencil, watercolor, oil, or animation—then explores the techniques, styles and subjects of the various artists.

The **Collector's Series** was inspired by, and designed for, the serious art enthusiast.

Hardcover, 144 pages, 10-1/4" x 13-3/4"

Beginners Art Series

The **Beginners Art Series** is a great way to introduce children to the wonderful world of art. Designed for ages 6 and up, this popular series helps children develop strong tactile and visual skills while they have a lot of fun! Each book explores a different medium and features exciting projects with simple step-by-step instructions and illustrations.

Paperback, 64 pages, 8-3/8" x 10-7/8"

Artist's Library Series

Serious instruction for serious artists—that's what the **Artist's Library Series** is all about! The books in this series can help both beginning and advanced artists expand their creativity, conquer technical obstacles, and investigate new media. Each book explores the materials and methods of a specific medium and includes step-by-step demonstrations, helpful tips, and comprehensive instructions.

The books of the **Artist's Library Series** are helpful additions to any artist's reference library.

Paperback, 64 pages, 6-1/2" x 9-1/2"